Stephen Boyce

The Blue Tree

Indigo Dreams Publishing

First Edition: The Blue Tree
First published in Great Britain in 2019 by:
Indigo Dreams Publishing
24, Forest Houses
Cookworthy Moor
Halwill
Beaworthy
Devon
EX21 5UU

www.indigodreams.co.uk

Stephen Boyce has asserted his right under the Copyright, Designs and Patents Act 1988 to be identified as the author of this work.
© Stephen Boyce 2019

ISBN 978-1-912876-12-9

British Library Cataloguing in Publication Data. A CIP record for this book can be obtained from the British Library.

This book is sold subject to the condition that it shall not, by way of trade or otherwise, be lent, re-sold, hired out, or otherwise circulated without the author's and publisher's prior consent in any form of binding or cover other than that in which it is published and without a similar condition including this condition being imposed on the subsequent purchaser.

Designed and typeset in Palatino Linotype by Indigo Dreams.
Cover image by Sioban Boyce.
Printed and bound in Great Britain by 4edge Ltd.

Papers used by Indigo Dreams are recyclable products made from wood grown in sustainable forests following the guidance of the Forest Stewardship Council.

In memory of my parents

And there, among the trees and their shadows, not understood, speaking a forgotten tongue, old dreads and formless awes and fascinations discover themselves...
Edward Thomas
The Heart of England

But I, all day, I heard an angel crying:
"Hurt not the trees."
Charlotte Mew

Acknowledgements

Thanks are due to the editors of the following magazines and anthologies in which some of these poems first appeared: *The Curlew; The Fenland Reed; The High Window; The Interpreter's House; Magma; Poetry & All That Jazz; Poetry Folio 70 (Kent & Sussex Poetry Society); Days Begin… (Wivenbooks 2015); Towards the Light (Kapaju Books 2018); Map: Poems After William Smith's Geological Map of 1815 (Worple 2015); The Tree Line: Poems for Trees, Woods & People (Worple 2017); Ver Poets competition anthology 2017; Wilfred Owen Association Journal.*

The Lone Tree of Loos was published by Somewhen in 2014 in a limited edition printed at Badger Press fine art printmaking studio, Bishops Waltham, Hampshire.

Early Fall and *Low Road* were commissioned by St Barbe Museum & Art Gallery, Lymington, to accompany the exhibition Under the Greenwood. *Earthwork* resulted from a collaboration with artist Kate Theodore for 10 Days | Creative Collisions 2013 and was published in *Yard & Metre*.

My special thanks go to Sophie Cunningham Dawe, visual artist, whose work inspired a number of these poems, for her spirit of collaboration and experiment; and to Sasha Dugdale to whom I'm particularly indebted for her expert, gentle and generous advice.

CONTENTS

TRIANGULATION

The Lone Tree of Loos 11
Escapement 12
Triangulation 13
Sturm und Drang 14
Outliers 15
Early Fall 16
Memorial with Dog 17
A Karaoke of the Night 18
Going Beyond 19
The Universe of Late Memory 20
Geological Survey 21
The Eleventh Hour 22
Refuge 23
The Vessel in Mind 24
Seasoned 25
The Dee in November 26

TRAVELLING COMPANIONS

William Walker, Diver, on Saving Winchester Cathedral from Risk of Collapse 1906-1911 29
Travelling Companions 30
P.S. 31
The Beekeeper's Wife 32
Everlasting 34
On Entering Duncliffe Wood 35
Cuts Both Ways 36
Corn Cockles 38

Frank Hurley's Negatives 39
Pendulum 40
His Mother Anointed, Bruges 1922 41
The Last September 42
Watching 'The Jewel in the Crown' 43
Low Road 44
What the Wazir Knew 45

THE BLUE TREE

To His Fingertips 49
Landfall 50
Choughs 51
Building Bridges 52
Under the Sun 53
Kintsugi 54
Flutter 56
Static 57
Earthwork 58
Morning Glory 60
Emerging from Rainforest 61
Heatwave 62
The Blue Tree 63
Shangri-La 64
Anniversary Waltz 65
How Spring Came 66
Woodland Pietà 68
A Peal for Wilfred Owen (4 November 2018) 70
Finishing Sentences 71
Notes 73

The Blue Tree

Triangulation

The Lone Tree of Loos

What matters is not that this landmark was a singleton,
self-sown, a range-finder they took pot shots at
over the barbed wire, in what became for them no-man's-land.

What matters is not that its scarred limbs would cradle
for three days or more the body of an officer
machine-gunned while raising his country's standard there.

What matters is not the million other trees of Flanders
felled for duckboards and ammunition boxes,
nor the Chinese labourers alongside lumberjacks and foresters.

What matters is not the name – *einsamer Baum, arbre solitaire* –
nor the remnants, the museum pieces,
the replanting eighty years on, the rooting in earth-memory.

What matters, beyond the white algebra of these cemeteries,
is this one wild cherry – 'loveliest of trees…'

Escapement

I came into the kitchen and the clock was ticking:
you had wound it again into the present tense,

into the fixity of each tooth-clicking second,
sweep of each minute, hour coiled upon hour,

so that we'd act in the moment and that instant
would be shuttered by a circle of numerals,

the matte face no place for pause or reflection;
and what we did now would be done for all time,

no regret, no hesitation, no winding it back,
no parallax error, and everything aligned

in the beat of a heart – like the sudden opening
of a bud beside the straits of Penang,

coinciding precisely with the arrival,
at last, of the slow train to Berrylands.

Triangulation

Duncliffe rises from the vale, the woodland
lying across its contours like a piecrust.
Mapless I take my bearings from a stand
of oak, a windbreak of yellow poplar, two
Scots pine – trees as waymarkers. Trees also
as trig points of the heart, like this immense
beech whose wide arc gives line of sight
to Leith Hill, soft landings among husks
and leaves; a maple counts off the seasons
on a colour-wheel of young love – love green,
love golden, love bleeding – while all along
the field's edge hips and haws mark exact
co-ordinates of rapture, and yew's soft red
berries measure one too many winter deaths.

Sturm und Drang

So much wind, all bluster and rampage,
the pummelling of fists on the roof,
rain that hisses and would pit the glass,
trees shouldered aside, birds hurled askew.

This fallen chestnut, some seasons down,
occupies the space beside the footpath
like a slaughtered rhino, its grey carcass
sinks imperceptibly into the ground.

This is what we'll come to, catching
the storm in a net, emptying the ocean
with a shell, lying down to die among
fallen lumber with the sound of the wind

rushing, the sound of the surf pounding,
and rain, teeming, thrashing, teeming.

Outliers

The day a wandering sheep ate our map
as we ploughed into wind on Moel y Plas –

and, skirting the mountain, we found our way
back to the car park, shrugged off the rain,

made it at last to the hotel, bathed, rested,
eased our aching limbs – you rescued

from thirty-five years of memory the name
of the farmer, our neighbour at Llanarmon,

just as the waitress (that same man's daughter)
described with what they call a lilt – softer

here than down south – her family home, sheep
scattered among bracken, the exposed scarp

and how Cynthia Lennon dropped in at the farm.

Early Fall

Enter the forest with a cautious tread,
the way you've stepped into this poem.

Be alert to the rustle of leaves –
something small startled in the undergrowth,

brushwood sifting an unexpected breeze.
Listen for a lone crow calling.

Breast the darkness along a track
no longer beaten – you may be lucky,

you may find a way back. Balk, if you must,
at discarded beer cans and bottles,

hesitate at outcrops of fungus,
let the spores settle deep in your lungs.

And if a firecrest fidgets in the canopy,
look to the sky where glistening particles

wait in their billions to moisten the green.
This is the moment you'll find yourself

peering through the ghostly shadow
of a plunging figure – skydiver,

space-walker, fallen angel – someone lost
whose immaculate wings would not open.

Memorial with Dog
i.m. MF

I count myself well versed in trees,
but this one's new to me, *Magnolia
Soulangeana Alba Superba*,

its roots, they say, Chinese
from Buddhist temple gardens
in Sichuan and in Yunnan.

With my O level Latin I unravel:
Magnolia after Pierre Magnol,
botanist (died 1715);

Soulangeana after Soulange-Bodin,
plantsman (died 1846), who bred
the saucer magnolia, tulip tree

of suburban English gardens;
Alba Superba, 'splendid white',
the variety you chose, Michael,

cyclist, theatre lover, naturist
(died 2011), who planted your own
memorial tree around which

the dog now runs wild, wondering
where you've gone, and why
these velvet buds are opening

into china bowls in which the rain
has poured a small libation.

A Karaoke of the Night

Music from the all-night disco
        echoes
across the valley, the way
        the mistral
staggers down alleyways, rattles the *Pins*
        Parasols
or ripples over clay-tiled roofs,
        catapulting
off telephone wires to coil itself around
        our balcony.
As day slopes through the shutters
        the beat's still there,
insistent, troubling, hard to shift,
        like the sand
that fell with yesterday's rain. I give up
        on sleep.
My head is filled with a new lexicon
        of riffs,
a din of pulses that shoves its way
        to the brim
of my lips, and hangs about all day.

Going Beyond

It's a kind of cliché – the view between curtains,
a reflection in a mirror, an archway's stark
geometry of sun and shade; in the landscape,
overhanging branches or the line of a road
that narrows into the distance – a frame,
a point of focus. The simple alignment
of water and skyline enchants the eye,
fixes the scene, so we follow cliff paths
round headlands and inlets till we arrive
at whatever defines the horizon, the edge
of things, limit of our comprehending.
We stand barefoot, heels anchored in sand,
toes tipping the ocean back and forth, as we scan
beyond the bounds of what we think we possess.

The Universe of Late Memory

The further out she travelled in the great field of stars, the more those memories escaped into the vacuum of night: all the twinkling, winking detail of names and dates and places, faces that came and went, and came again; the bank clerks, sea captains, end-of-pier turns, good-time soldiers chewing black shellac 78s in the colonial club – everyone who ever thrilled and appalled her – hovering in the depths of space, out of reach and drawing her back.

And always that lingering shadow – the one whose silhouette was so familiar to her – that peered around constellations, slid watchful between galaxies; the one that seemed to nudge her deeper, under, over, far beyond the edge of the edgeless universe – that would, in time, enfold her in its long dark arms.

Geological Survey

I unfold the map and spread it before you.
You run your hand over the surface:

the whorls of your fingertips are dusted
with a patina of chalk and anthracite,

traces of pumice, the ground bones of fish;
your thumb is stained with iron, your hands

smell of molluscs, the peaty odour of ferns.
It's as if they've been lying in wait for us

as we lean over the table with the fondness
of long-layered strata, shoulder to shoulder.

My knuckles rise like outcrops of granite,
the moons of my fingernails contain oceans,

fault lines cross my palm with seams of ore.
You put your finger to my lips to hush me

and I taste fathoms of salt. At my temple
I hear the wingbeats of pterosaurs.

How have we not lived like this before?

The Eleventh Hour

A bugler sounds the last post as starlight spills from this rusting memorial box – eleven cubed – and I recall how a friend used to say that other people's lives are always more interesting. But, as the standard is slowly lowered, I find I am thinking only how different and alike our lives may be, how the box of one heart can be filled with broken and bloody knives while another is full to the brim with a heaven of brilliant, indelible stars.

Refuge

What washes up in the forest is no less
a wonder than the flotsam of oceans.

Take this skeleton of an upturned ark
stranded among a reach of ash trees,

beached in leaf litter, its ribs and spars
secured by a rigging of twiggy larch,

tangles of plaited honeysuckle, all
leaning in as though wanting to give ear

to silence, breathe the wood's cool must.
Some Crusoe surely built this, laid limbs

against a fallen ridgepole, wove vines
and brushwood, spread out a bed of brash,

learned how stillness is a state of mind,
here where things slither, drip and flinch.

The Vessel in Mind

She said 'make me a vessel for your love.'
I thought outrigger, galleon, ocean-going junk.

She had in mind a cup made of bone china,
steady in the slight well of its saucer.

Seasoned

Splitting logs, so much depends
on anvil, ground, arc and heft,
timing of fall and whether the wood
is seasoned enough not to resist
the iron hurled into sycamore
or the dark heartwood of yew.

Stacking logs is all a matter
of split, weight, angle of wedge,
degree of purchase and whether
the wood is seasoned enough
not to shift: laburnum jammed,
pear on edge in the cradle beneath.

A labour of making, not unmaking,
of hewing the sawn log into angular
units, building a wall of ripening
chestnut, apple, thuja, lime – fire-
seed to spark and fuel to flame:
heat and light in their season.

The Dee in November

Dim ond calon lân all ganu
Canu'r dydd a chanu'r nos.

We stood in the sun at Llangollen
as the standard bearers lowered
their flags. And, after the singing
of Calon Lân, as the red wreaths
were being laid, Jones by Jones,
Llewelyn by Lloyd, Owen, Price,
all the Robertses and Thomases,
the dead were recited, recalled,
remembered, to the low reverent
incantation of water falling, falling
over the grey, glistening stone.

None but a pure heart can sing,
sing day and night.
Calon Lân, *Daniel James (1848-1920)*

Travelling Companions

William Walker, Diver, on Saving Winchester Cathedral from Risk of Collapse 1906-1911

Twenty feet down in the peat, the drowned and deadbeat
timbers, I have laboured, tethered to a line of pumped air,
weighed down by lead in my boots, the passing years,
sediment of chalk. I'm blinded now by visions of flame,
after the godless dark, the peat, the drowned and deadbeat
timbers.
      Yes, let's talk of God, praised with gargoyles, corbels,
painted bosses, wreaths and fiery devils (visions of flame) –
what does He know of passing years, sediment of chalk?
Will He see 25,000 bags of concrete, 900,000 bricks, five years
in the godless dark and pumped air to shore up His house,
its gargoyles, corbels and bosses?
                                  Better not to think like this.
Best unplug the air, remove the boots – drowned, deadbeat –
lay down the helmet of copper and brass, its visions of flame,
a stone's throw from the last remains of Cnut the Great.

Travelling Companions
for RJH

Joining you some way into your journey
I find myself on desert tracks, following

camel trains and silk roads, among Sufi
and Tuareg, wanderers in the cradle

of being – simple lives finely tuned,
seeking and giving – where a goat is worth

more than gems, where there is honour
among traders, among neighbours, even

among poets, where the life of the nomad
is an act of devotion, where the landscape

holds no distraction and a moment
of stillness is worth a lifetime of struggle.

P.S.

Am enclosing a photo I thought you'd enjoy.
Two oak trees at the edge of a wood, outliers,
close as lovers – so that, seen from afar,
you'd believe there was just the one trunk.
I took it last Thursday, 1st of December,
as the hoar frost began to recede. I think
you can see there's a drizzle of leaves
released as the ice loses grip. Soon the trees
will be bare, just a fretwork of twigs against
grey winter skies. But, for now, that cinnamon
colour that's staining the grass sits so well
beside bark and the greeny-grey lichen,
rays of sunlight slant in the mist.
                              The scene
was so peaceful I couldn't help thinking of you,
the stillness you taught me, though I've yet
to perfect it, the patience I saw in the way
that trees grow – not resignation, but strength
in the flow and the cycle of things. Even
an oak that's stood here for centuries
is on its way through, you said, doing its bit,
offering itself, for shelter or shade, moving on
in its acorns and galls – just as you did,
dear friend, though in your case all too soon.

The Beekeeper's Wife

The beekeeper of Peski
cannot leave his hives,
will not leave his bees.
There are tears in his eyes.

His wife, Svetlana,
has grey hairs, he says.
The beekeeper can't explain
what she means to him;
she is there behind him,
with her grey hairs
and a catch in her throat.

The bees are there,
the industrious bees
which he cannot leave.
The neighbours have all gone,
all moved away.

This poor Ukraine is broken into pieces,
says Anatoly, beekeeper of Peski.

He will not leave the bees.
They have tears in their hives.
He can't explain
what the grey hairs
and the bees mean to him.

Ukraine is there behind him,
with tears in her eyes
and a catch in her throat.

His wife, Svetlana,
cannot explain the neighbours,
the tears, or yet the bees.
The beekeeper's wife
is moving away
with bees in her throat,
her eyes broken into pieces.

Everlasting

Forty years on, settled in the jar with a cork lid,
hardly a petal has fallen from these strawflowers

since the day you wove them round the brim of your hat
and stepped into the garden of our marriage.

Even the colours have endured, deep carmine, gold,
soft pink and yellow, and as I bring the jar up close

I feel the warmth of sunlight, taste the dry waft
of stubble after harvest. I place a flowerhead

on the palm of my hand, a brittle cluster – rosette –
of petals, whose kiss remains as light as breath.

On Entering Duncliffe Wood

What is it the wood keeps to itself?

Some story of Domesday scribes, po-faced,
foraging for stinkhorn and death cap?

The words that rooks overheard
of Cromwell's so-called parley?
                         A tale
of abandoned babies perhaps, here
where stumps and roots are draped
in a plush of moss and look more
like the claws of dragons.
                         Or is it to do
with the nuns, how they spoke
of the shameless fern unfurling its bishop's crook?

The twitch and stagger of the beech tree's
dangling rope, is it that?
                         I tell you –
a few steps in and your heart will start
at the crack of a stick, at the woodpecker's
echoing 'knock, knock-knock',
at the creaking tree, the distant shriek.

Cuts Both Ways

Perhaps a breadknife
came to hand more readily.
Perhaps he thought its serrated edge
more threatening
when touching the flesh of the neck.

For when he and his mate
– there's always a mate standing by –
shoved the kid between the chainlink fence
and the concrete lockup,
threat was mainly what was intended.

So, wielding a breadknife
while glaring into his face
eyeball to eyeball,
crushing his back against the wall,
snarling, calling him all the foul names
he could conjure,
was his way of summoning a spell,
a kind of evil magic
that would bend the boy to his will.

The knife did its subtle work
though they saw little of each other
in the days that followed.

And that face is a blur now,
not much more than a shadow,
so that it's difficult to recall if this
was the same burly lad
whose dad

had changed the family name
from Feldmann to Field,
and whom a pack of others
– with their bystanders –
once pissed on in a dank alleyway
on their way home from school.

Corn Cockles
for Marthe de Méligny (Maria Boursin)

    Lying in the bath
with not much more than his head and feet
breaking the surface

and his legs straight as train tracks,
he thought of Bonnard's wife.

                        The way that,
catching her at her toilette,
       with or without a towel,
and perhaps the afternoon sunshine
       at the window,

a vase on the dressing table,

that dapper man
       revealed so much of them both
to the world they shied away from.

And how the room and the water,
the sunlight and the corn cockles,
       contained
in their scintillating colour

all that the world could offer of passion,
       of joy,
made real by his eye,
       made constant by his brushwork.

Frank Hurley's Negatives

Imagine, every one of these plates we'll weigh,
hold up to snow-light with fur-mittened hands,
cull as we crouch on the ice.

Every one of five hundred scenes – the ghostly dogs,
white beards frosted black, the night sky pallid
above a dark ice-shelf – every one we'll test
against the freezing point of truth, boiling point of beauty.

Those we save we'll lock away in boxes soldered shut
for posterity – or return to Blighty.

Those we agree to discard
we'll shatter – shivers of glass scattered over pack ice
that, in time, will crush and swallow itself,
and the glazed memory of itself,
just as its groaning floes overwhelm our ship,
here in the Weddell Sea.
                        This sheer white table,
in the shadow of the yardarm, beneath its cobwebby rigging,
is where we'll kneel and make our choices.

We will not despair, we will not presume.
And this will be both pledge and proof.

Pendulum

We drove the turnpike down to Long Cross,
                two German biker girls riding ahead of us
Indian file. And the one behind swayed left,
      sashayed right, glided side to side as a child would
– or a gull lolling on a warm updraft.

           We were going somewhere as yet unknown
following the line of the trees, sweep of the hills,
              the contours of our faltering hearts
to where a new life was heading out to meet us.

           I can't remember now if the bikers turned off
at the town or gunned their machines, opened
              the throttle, tore away into the distance,
but they left us clear road, the blue sky of winter.

           And I knew from the tilt of her head, the grace
of her shoulder, how the young woman smiled
              like the painted sun on an antique clock,
as she swung to and fro, tracing
            joyous half-moons from the tick to the tock.

His Mother Anointed, Bruges 1922

Through the window of the perfumery
the assistant in her neat maquillage
watches a small goose-gaggle of schoolgirls
scurry across the cobbles beneath the Belfry.
Notre Dame aux Epines, afternoon exeat.

The doorbell tinkles on its springy coil,
the girls giggle and shush. Slender fingers
trace the mirrored vitrine's bevelled edges:
Dior, Lanvin, Chanel – and here Arys,
by appointment to the queen of Norway,
also to the royal house of Spain:
ice and fire at one in frosted Lalique glass.

The bottle unstoppered, its scent released,
a pale wrist is kissed with the moistened stem.
L'Amour dans Le Coeur.
                        Some decades later,
a small advertising card too precious
to be lost – a podgy art nouveau Cupid
paying court to a girl with hair like yours –
all the evidence of your heart's first fluttering.

The Last September
after Elizabeth Bowen

She'd never come out through a pass, looked down
on distinct white cities with no smoke.
She had never been in a tunnel for more
than five minutes, she'd heard there were tunnels
in which you could suffocate. She'd never
seen anything larger than she could imagine.
She wanted, she said, to see backgrounds
without bits taken out of them by Holy Families;
small black trees running up and down white hills.
She thought the little things would be important:
trees with electric lights growing out of them.
She did not care for views, did not want adventures.
She wanted to go wherever the war hadn't,
wanted to see something only she would remember.

Watching 'The Jewel in the Crown'

Daphne Manners is wearing round tortoiseshell
specs like the ones you wore in that photo Dad took

as you nestled beneath the paper parasol,
in love. She has on a flower-print sundress like yours

as she lounges on the verandah at Mayapore
sipping gin fizz with 'aunt' Lili Chatterjee.

Perhaps at the convent in Bruges the other girls
teased you, that old lie about men not making passes,

because I've seen the snaps of you without your glasses,
on the beach, with the collie dog, on the pillion,

but that was before he proposed, before the rains
came, making the air in the hills smell sweet

and misting up your lenses, so that it was harder
to identify the men from the Bibighar Gardens.

But I forget, that wasn't you, you had moved back
to the house in Berrylands where, every so often,

a parcel arrived in the post from Darjeeling
and, having settled the child, you'd sit in the kitchen

tasting your tea and dreaming of the moment
he'd walk through the door, kitbag on his shoulder,

camera in hand, and the monsoon in his eyes.

Low Road
after *Low Road* by Elizabeth Magill (oil on canvas 2012)

It wasn't clear to me that you knew who I was.
Even so you seemed saddened when I left.
And more than sad. That's what made it so hard,
both of us bereft, my heart heavier
with each wearying sweep of the wipers
as I drove the low road back to where I started,

windscreen crazed with patterns of rain, smeared and gone,
smeared and gone like the questions in your eyes,
the trees a tracery of blood vessels
or route-maps, blurred, indecipherable,
arching over the tarmac and white lines
as I followed the valley road into half-light.

What the Wazir Knew

Whether it was superstition, custom or convention,
Count Bronowsky knew of it and counselled the young woman
to sit awhile before setting off for Pankot.

As the Count was also aware, Chekhov
has Ranevskaya do the same, as the old house is locked up
and the axes can be heard in the orchard.

He too had sat – or paused at least – before departing
and in that moment of calm remembered the keys,
a gift left on the sideboard, a message to be delivered.

But mostly he recollected himself, detached himself
from the place he was leaving, connected
with his destination, weighed the task before him.

He drew breath in tranquility, a purer deeper breath
to sustain him on the journey, feed him afresh on arrival
– wherever he might be.

Yet the wazir's gammy leg, they said, was the result
of just such a pause, but for which he might have avoided
being blown up, would not have lost an eye.

That was when he'd learnt it was all about knowing when –
and also how long – to wait before setting out,
before closing the door behind you.

The Blue Tree

To His Fingertips

When he slipped climbing out of a poplar tree
    and slid the length of the coarse rope,
he was twelve or thirteen or thereabouts,
    and his mind was filled only with the pain
of the eight fingers whose flesh was ripped to the bone,
    not the loss of their singular identifiers.
And he swore more violently than ever he had before
    as he righted himself and stared at his hands,
where the skin was burned and lifted,
    and he found he could no longer discern
what he thought of as himself, or touch
    the world that surrounded him.
Nor could he be traced in the wasteland of brambles
    where he lived for the following months,
while an assortment of ointments and balms was applied
    and, from the sheen of his new skin,
there emerged the same set of fingerprints,
    their unique pattern of arches, loops and whorls
legible now as he lifted them from the inkpad
    and pressed them firmly to the paper.

Landfall
for Brian

Like Dali's silver shoes
walking on water,
the catamaran we christened *Cadaques*
bobbed and dipped on the boat pond,
her cotton sail surrendering to not much breeze
as you brought her into port for me.

Choughs

At the cliff's edge
        we crouched among tussocks,
peaty humps
        plump as church kneelers.

The birds came and went
        above, below, above again,
skirred in and out
        of a sea-facing scarp,

rose on the updraughts
        – their red legs dangling –
steadied then turned
        in the salty blast,

before floating away
        like wodges of paper –
gossipy letters,
        set loose by fire,

carrying their secrets
        in smouldering char,
to wedge in a cleft of the rock
        or drift on the wind,

too far out and long gone.

Building Bridges

She was resolute as the Pont Valentré
        or Brooklyn Bridge,
upright, load-bearing – sturdy piers,
solid beam – the here and now, at a stroke.

He was all arc and span, bowstring, tension
        and flex, a reminder
of Millau, even that undulating cat's cradle
        over the Firth of Forth.

She was anchored, emphatic, a colossus,
        a hub. She endured.
He, the elegant parenthesis
        of engineered ribs and cables.
He moved with the wind,
all loose articulation from shoulder to wrist,

as when, finally, he was close enough
to reach across the divide, place a hand
        at her cheek, embrace her,
and, like the crossings of Cherrapunji,
their permanently entwined roots
        became a living web,
an arc of moon made whole by the water beneath.

Under the Sun

The tan my dad acquired on the Burmese front
in '45 – a tawny hide intensified
in years to come by soaked-up greenhouse sun,
trips to the Med – he passed it down the line.

My skin, too, turns brown with ease. I feel a hint
of sunlight warm my face and know its tint
will redden, soon to bronze. *You're looking well,*
they say, *been somewhere nice?*
                                          And that is all
it takes for me to think of him in a packed train –
Calcutta to Lahore and back again –
or at the battery west of Arakan
cajoling ranks of sepoys. It was then
the sun appeared to blink, momently. A whisper
of breeze. Unaccustomed silence. Rainfall.

Months later he was home and dressed in civvies,
nut brown throughout the hardest winter,
and all the bitter cold of England in the fifties.
So he went back to work, and I to school.

Kintsugi

We linger over breakfast
and time and again
your mother's attention
      is snagged
by a hairline crack
on the inside of her cup
running through the wings
      of a butterfly,
tea-stained now
      after so much use.
On the outside of the cup
the crack divides
      a spray of violets
where she sets her lips.
When you ask her
if it affects the taste
      of her tea
she answers
      Not to my mind.

And light filters through
the porcelain
      with a soft sheen
everywhere except
      the line of that crack,
as her mind flits
like a sparrow on the feeder:
This cup has a crack in it,
      she announces.
Yes, you say
for the third time

in as many minutes,
it's been there a while.
> *It's quite old.*

And I hear you trying
to mend that
> precious fracture

with a seam of
> lacquered gold.

Flutter

It had begun with sweet palpitation
as if, on entering the chambers,
the blood gulped for oxygen,
recognised the moment for what it was –
delicious risk, a once-in-a-lifetime
winner-takes-all chance to beat the house,
to stake the lot on finding love.

Eventually it was a tale of stents
and shunts, of ventricles kept open
ballooned in hope, of furred-up plumbing
bypassed to keep it pumping,
somehow, with tripwires to jolt
the flabby muscle into life again,
some semblance of rhythm, however faint.

And in the shadow of such heart-stopping
moments, he caught the quick glint
of her eyes, felt a settling and shifting,
or the sudden swerve of an insect in flight.
This was what he lived for now,
the transparency of wings, strong enough
to lift him once more into the light.

Static

Perhaps nothing here is still. Whatever appears so
has shifted even before I turn: the mirrored boat
that drifts soundlessly into the canal bank on another's
passing wash, a fringe of rosebay willowherb
whose seed-sheaths split, unfurl, lift off out of sight –
to start the whole circular business afresh.

And nothing occupies a space equal to itself,
not the water that shrugs as the lock gate shuts,
the comfrey stealing along the towpath's hem,
nor the curtained narrowboat whose bikes, plants and prams
sprawl the length of its roof – even the hot-fingered sun
reaches up my neck to stir the finer hairs.

The gravel, too, now lifted and scuffed by tread and tyre,
shifts and, as it does so, emits a wheezing electricity.

Earthwork
for Kate Theodore

I picture you up to your biceps
in clay, a lone figure in an arid landscape,

the day already burning hot as you assemble,
reassemble

fragments of stone,
a fossilised shell, a petrified bone

prised from the mind
as much as the ground,

the red earth of Spain.
And, brushing dust from the crumbled remains,

you pause, wipe your arm on your brow
where sweat has now

sealed a pink-orange smear to the pores of your skin
like some ritual sign

or a hex on a gate.
And up to your waist in the half-dug pit,

you are every bit the digger and leveller,
scraper and shoveller,

so the spoil heap rises with each spadeful of waste
and you're keeping it moist

with fistfuls of water, smoothing the surface, getting a feel
for the form or the figure concealed

inside, the transcendent image your hands will expose,
the rose

in the rock –
or paring it back

layer by layer, breaking it down to the zillionth part,
to the particle of particles,

the definite article,
the science of life, the essence of art.

Morning Glory

Where the scalp was shaved to clean and stitch the wound,
below the crown's neat whorl, your hair has now re-grown.

A different head of hair, untameable and straggly, each fibril
twists and curls, savagely entwined like wild bramble

or the bindweed that's colonised our garden, that deceives us
with its trumpet flowers, their pert pretence of innocence.

Emerging from Rainforest

Hear the nine-note calling bird – all-night sentinel
among fig, myrtle and eucalyptus?

The moth, impatient tapper at windows,
forest dragon and orange-toed scratchy thing,

a lumpen frog gawping at the lit footpath – who cares?
What matters is the night, moonlight on the coast,

the ocean shelf where you and I have perched
in this moment of unadulterated peace.

For we have passed the stage of being mere creatures
– of habit or otherwise, and of ourselves –

we are sentient, placid, we have grown content
in our presentiment of the not-far-off,

to which almost everything seems to alert us
with echoes of that insistent nine-note summons.

Heatwave

I went outside to hose down the greenhouse
and top up the fish pond.

When I returned you had filled the room with moths
and a tall vase of moonlight.

The Blue Tree

The night the blue tree was struck by lightning,
its thicket of twigs absorbing the shock,
protecting its slender trunk, we had sat out late
in that sticky air, uncertain as to what
made us want to be there – the oppressive heat
of the house, a glint of moonlight on moths' wings,
an odd falling star? Or the want of company,
a desire to feel we had made amends?

The talk was of the here, the new, the now,
we did not venture into the past. The future
was masked by night. We let silences bloom,
as what had gone before rose and settled
in the blue tree's tangled thatch. Then the fork,
and jagged flashes lighting up the gorge.

Shangri-La

Because your son, my father, would not speak for shame
about the circumstances of your birth,
I went in search of you among the archives
and family papers. Not a trace.

Except a hand-written census record that declares you
'adopted son' of James, a 'letter carrier'.
And there it stops. Just ink, foxed paper,
a screen of pixels. No story.

And all I really want is for you to tell me
that your father, your true father,
was a man with small hands who enjoyed his garden,
read sometimes, was kindly.

And that your mother – birth mother – just possibly
made it to the Kunlun Mountains where they laid out rugs
on the river bank, brought peaches for her to eat
under the pearl and jade trees.

Anniversary Waltz

Count in cotton, in paper and in pearl,
in tooth-tested precious metal.

Count the breaths, the vows, the tears,
the tables laid for two, then three or four.

Then three, then two again. Count the rings
on fingers, phones and in the core of trees.

Count the falling leaves, the ticking clocks,
the beep of monitors, the drip, the drip, the drip.

And, before you part, count the countless kisses,
thrilling, tender, doting, dry – count

the rhythm of the halting heart.

How Spring Came

I had brought in queen wasps hibernating
in the soft tissue of logs. Unseen by us
they emerged in the warmth of the room where

I trapped them, returned them to cold night air.
We doused the fire, turned in and as I reached
for the light-switch a moth – common swift –

lifted off, disturbed from whatever dream
it was dreaming – of winking shadows,
the guttering seduction of a candle's flame.

*

The night I returned to you, the night I came
to lie beside you, a mischief of magpies
was heard gossiping, starlings scrabbled

beneath the eaves again, while you abandoned
thoughts of winter duvets – for a while –
and slid towards the centre of the bed,

that warm familiar dip in which our love
had come to rest, the nest we'd laboured
to construct, that held us till we woke to light.

*

Our bodies having given up the effort
of the day before, the room smelled sweet
as I slipped from the bed leaving you asleep.

It was one of those mornings when sound
carries through clear air – the diminuendo
of a plane making its final approach,

the wavefall of distant traffic. I let loose
the ladybirds, a score or more gathered
at our windowsill, my ears filled with wingbeats.

Woodland Pietà

Background left to right: The pale lance
of a larch sapling, snapped at the base,
stripped of its bark, pierces the shadow.
Then elder.
                   A holly tree so dark, crowned
with old man's beard, so wintry dank.
Stems of ash, seven ages of gash and healing,
       some bent to the ground,
              some still thrusting skyward.

In the foreground: a broken bough,
sweet chestnut perhaps, slant
and completely severed from the bole,
              leafless
in the cradle of a lower branch,
      its weight
draining into that slumped embrace.

A dead oak tree resembles forked lightning –
upturned – or writhing anguish pitched
       against sullen skies.

Far right: gnarled hazel rods
       tortured
by woody coils of honeysuckle.
An unidentified trunk
       in a ragged cloak of ivy.

In the far distance: A view of fields,
smoke from a cottage, village church.

Note also: How coppicing has opened
        the canopy,
how sunlight dapples the forest floor,
        how the men and women sit in its warm rays
                among stacked logs and lopped brash
        drinking from a flask.
How they have put their trust in spring.

A Peal for Wilfred Owen (4 November 2018)
for Vanessa Davis

The muscular Charolais are startled, as I am,
by flares and thunderous maroons in the 6 a.m. mist,
the darkness illuminated by twinkling frost
as our torch beams pass through the field
and we assemble on the bank of the Sambre-Oise canal,
one hundred years to the hour after the signal to cross,
the burst of gunfire from a farmhouse on the far side,
men slumped and dying on pontoons – then nothing
but silence.
               And yes, there must have been a lump
in the throat of the day, another day of negotiations,
endless bloody negotiations, when all that was needed
was a signing and an end.
                        What is there to say now,
each of us alone in a crowd of one hundred, alone
on the canal path with our own muddled thoughts?
Are we sad for them? Sorry for ourselves? Is it the loss?
Yes of course, it's always about what is lost. And pity, too –
he had it right, all is pity – as the light comes slowly
to silhouette the trees on the far bank, and the frost
reflects on the hide of those pallid cattle who browse
between pollarded willows.
                       As maybe they did
a week later when the postman stood at the door
and handed two letters to Owen's mother, the last
he wrote in the cellar of the forester's house
and the one from his CO announcing her son's death,
while all the bells rang out, all the bells rang out.

Finishing Sentences

Afterwards (it was hard to tell how much
time had passed), in recompense
we gave back the best of ourselves,

made a kind of parcel of our lives,
wrapped in the fine tissue of forgiveness
and a shiny layer of self-love,

tied it with a bow of hope, pulled tight.
We exchanged gifts then,
our hearts open as the spring rain

– so glad were we to have met again.
Now we walk an avenue of lime trees
towards a patch of sunlight

where, in our eagerness, words come tumbling
and we're finishing … *each other's sentence.*

Notes

The Eleventh Hour responds to the light installation, 'Box 459', commissioned by Winchester City Council and designed by AR Design Studio, to mark the centenary of the outbreak of the First World War. The dimensions of the box – an 1100mm steel cube – refer to the Armistice, and a powerful internal light source projects its shafts through 459 apertures representing the city's fallen soldiers.

William Walker, Diver, on Saving Winchester Cathedral from Risk of Collapse 1906-1911 – In the early 1900s, over 800 years after its construction, the East end of Winchester cathedral was found to be collapsing. A diver was required to replace the original timber piling which was below the water table. This laborious work was carried out by William Walker whose remarkable achievement is commemorated in the cathedral.

Frank Hurley's Negatives – Australian photographer Frank Hurley accompanied Ernest Shackleton's ill-fated Imperial Trans-Antarctic Expedition of 1914-1917. Their ship, *Endurance*, became trapped for 15 months in the pack ice of the Weddell Sea. During the winter of 1915, Hurley created over 500 pictures – large format glass plate negatives. When the loss of the ship became inevitable, and before they and the rest of the crew set off on an extraordinary journey of escape, Shackleton and Hurley selected 150 key images and destroyed the remainder.

Kintsugi – the Japanese art of repairing broken pottery with lacquer dusted or mixed with powdered gold or other precious metal – relates to the philosophy of "no mind" (無心 mushin), which encompasses the concept of non-attachment, acceptance of change and fate as aspects of human life.

Indigo Dreams Publishing Ltd
24, Forest Houses
Cookworthy Moor
Halwill
Beaworthy
Devon
EX21 5UU
www.indigodreams.co.uk